PR6061.U68 KUR

BIRDS OF PASSAGE

DATE DUE FOR RETURN

For Phillip ('Pee Wee') Weaver

HANIF KUREISHI

BIRDS OF PASSAGE

AMBER LANE PRESS

All rights whatsoever in this play are
strictly reserved and application for
performance, etc. should be made before
rehearsal to:

Sheila Lemon Limited,
Assets House,
17 Elverton Street,
London SW1P 2QG

No performance may be given unless a licence has been
obtained.

First published 1983 by
Amber Lane Press Ltd.,
9 Middle Way,
Oxford OX2 7HL

Typesetting and page make-up by
Midas Publishing Services Ltd., Oxford

Printed in Great Britain by
Cotswold Press Ltd., Oxford

ISBN 0 906399 48 3

CHARACTERS

DAVID	Dad, 57
AUDREY	Mum, 55
STELLA	their daughter, 28
PAUL	their son, 23
EVA	Audrey's sister, 50
TED	her husband, 50
ASIF	the lodger, 29

Birds of Passage was first performed at Hampstead Theatre, London, on 15th September 1983, with the following cast:

STELLA	Belinda Sinclair
PAUL	Neil Pearson
DAVID	Joe Melia
AUDREY	Jean Boht
EVA	Rowena Cooper
ASIF	Raad Rawi
TED	Roger Sloman

Director	Howard Davies
Designer	Sue Plummer

Certain changes to the text may have been made during rehearsal and after this edition went to press.

ACT ONE

SCENE ONE

PAUL *is playing the piano upstairs.* STELLA *comes on, carrying a suitcase.*

STELLA: [*calling*] Mum. [*Pause.*] Mum. Dad.
        [PAUL *begins to sing as he plays.*]
        Paul, can you stop that?
        [*He continues.*]
        Look what I've brought you.
        [*He stops. Pause. He continues.*]
        Duty-free.
        [*He stops. He appears.*]

PAUL: [*singing at her*] "I ain't good-looking babe, and I don't dress fine—"

STELLA: Aren't they here? I rang to say I was coming.

PAUL: And they went out. [*singing*] "But I'm a travelling woman with a travelling mind." You've come all this way. Chelsea isn't it?

STELLA: I've been in Paris for two months.

PAUL: What's it like? I've never even been on a plane.
        [*She indicates to him and he goes to her. He hugs her.*]
        Love your clothes, your smell, everything. Kiss you.
        [*But he licks her.*]

STELLA: Bloody fool.
        [*She produces a bottle of whisky from her bag.*]

PAUL: Here. You obviously love your brother. [*He bangs a nearby chair enthusiastically.*] Relax. They've only gone up Sydenham Station in Auntie Eva's car.

STELLA: It's so long since I've been here.

PAUL: Eight months.

STELLA: Do they resent that? Oh why should they? Sydenham's a leaving place.

PAUL: Oh yes.

STELLA: You'll get out of South London won't you, Paul?

PAUL: 'Course, but where is there?

STELLA: When I was a kid and had 'flu I lay on the sofa and looked at the wallpaper for hours. It'll still be marked where I scribbled on it. Sorry I haven't had time to ask you up for lunch.

PAUL: How is being in South London like being hit with a fish?

STELLA: I don't know. How is it like being hit with a fish?

PAUL: It keeps you awake, in a funny kind of way. Those lunches are a high point with me. Clever people dropping in. Been busy at the language school, I expect. I have seen you, Stella.

[*He gives her the bottle. She drinks.*]

I've watched you.

[*She hands back the bottle. He looks at it.*]

Lipstick.

STELLA: Have you been following me?

PAUL: How did you get it inside the rim?

[*He licks round the rim.*]

When I saw you, Stel, you were drinking a drink with cucumbers in. This was at the Mozambique Club. You remember? I would have asked you for money.

STELLA: You unemployed?

PAUL: 'Course. But if I could get work I'd run ten miles. I want more than a job.

STELLA: D'you know what you want?

PAUL: You left the ol' Mozambique with a foreigner who had on a green suit and sweat on his head. You walked right past me. I could have put my hand up your skirt.

STELLA: You didn't.

PAUL: You didn't seem anything to do with me. You could have been anyone. I have envied you. And there you were in the Mozambique, having a hectic time in leopard-skin trousers, with a face as human as a potato. Who was the old man?

STELLA: How did you get into the Mozambique?

PAUL: Toilet window. You too?

STELLA: You appear in those places now?

PAUL: 'Bout once a week I have a bit of fun up London. Rest of the time I'm roaming round here.

STELLA: Who's behind this?

PAUL: A friend of mine. Asif. He specialises in leading people into trouble.

STELLA: [*picking up her bag*] I'll put this upstairs.

PAUL: Are you intending to sleep in the same bed as the new lodger they've just gone to pick up? He's got your room. He's attractive, but it's early days.

STELLA: Who is he?

PAUL: He's a quiet student, at Imperial College. Mum told you she's being laid off, didn't she?

STELLA: I love her more than anyone.

PAUL: Late.

STELLA: I thought about her every day in France.

PAUL: She bores us all to bleedin' death.

STELLA: What's the lodger's name?
[*Noise outside.*]

DAVID: [*off*] Get round, Audrey, and open that door. I'll twist this round, twist this round and hold it up. [*He strains.*] Yes! Now!

EVA: [*off*] You're on the front of my shoe, David, and you didn't say we'd be moving furniture!

DAVID: [*off*] Out the way you useless woman!

STELLA: Who is he?
[PAUL *snatches the bottle from her and swigs.*]
You bloody little animal.

AUDREY: [*off*] I'm not doing any more.

DAVID: [*off*] Oh yes you are.

PAUL: Don't look scared. We're family.

STELLA: Auntie Eva with them?

PAUL: Yeah.

ASIF: [*off*] Mr Bareham.

DAVID: [*off*] Asif, what? What?

ASIF: [*off*] I think the paint's coming off the wall just here.

DAVID: [*off*] The fucking house is round our ankles. [*shouting*] Paul! Are you in there Paul?

PAUL: [*shouting*] I'm in here, yes.

DAVID: [*off, shouting*] If you're in there, then get out here, you bloody fool!

> [*And* PAUL *goes out.* STELLA *prepares herself. Then they all enter, carrying* ASIF's *trunk.* EVA *is well-dressed.* AUDREY *sees* STELLA.]

AUDREY: My baby's here.

> [*She lets go of her bit of the trunk.*]

PAUL: [*taking the weight*] Jesus, Mum.

> [*They put the trunk down.* AUDREY *embraces* STELLA. ASIF *and* PAUL *shake hands.*]

STELLA: [*to* AUDREY] Mum, when did you get glasses?

AUDREY: Hasn't she got a nice coat on?

EVA: [*fingering the coat*] Hallo, my love. Tough leather's back in is it?

STELLA: Auntie Eva.

PAUL: [*to* ASIF] You got here, eh?

EVA: [*to* AUDREY] Remind me to give you my skunk-skin hat.

PAUL: [*to* ASIF] You're miles from everything, you know that?

AUDREY: There's a shopping centre. A canal, and—

DAVID: He wants to study, not rumba.

> [ASIF *nods.*]
>
> I know the feeling.

AUDREY: [*indicating* STELLA] My only daughter, Stella.

STELLA: Hallo.

EVA: [*looking at the label on the trunk*] Defence Housing, Karachi. Pakistan. You're Pakistani.

AUDREY: Let's push this out of the way. Paul.

> [AUDREY *and* PAUL *push the trunk out of the way.*]

EVA: [*to* ASIF] What a long way to have come. You're the first Pakistani I've met. We hear a lot about them.

AUDREY: Quite a lot.

EVA: I could have carried that trunk to Brazil. I wonder why I feel so exhilarated today?

DAVID: To be over here and out of your own house. Ted getting you down more than usual?

EVA: No. Yes. Yes.

DAVID: In this society we hate change. We make no provision for it. We see it negatively, as disruption.

ASIF: [*interested*] Why?

DAVID: We cling onto things. [*to* EVA] Leave him.

EVA: I'm fond of our garden. You haven't seen the rock garden.

DAVID: I'm not moved by rocks.

EVA: You never come over now, neither of you.

DAVID: You're welcome here. If it makes life easier, Eva.

EVA: It's a long time since you've been so nice to me.

DAVID: I don't mean to be.

PAUL: [*to* ASIF, *brandishing a coin*] Heads or tails! A quid! Heads?

AUDREY: [*to* ASIF] Are you feeling peckish, duck?

ASIF: Sorry?

EVA: He's ravishing, I bet—
            [PAUL *tosses the coin and holds it covered on the back of his hand.*]

PAUL: [*uncovering it*] You've won son. As always.

EVA: [*to* ASIF] I'll get him a nice corned-beef sandwich.
            [EVA *exits.*]

DAVID: [*to* STELLA] Painful to be home?

STELLA: Why should I rush here? You usually only want me to vote at one of your meetings.

AUDREY: [*to* ASIF] Sit down.

DAVID: [*to* ASIF] Make yourself comfortable.

AUDREY: [*to* ASIF] David made us all join his Labour Party. So when he wants to pass a motion we all have to go and vote. I usually drop off because I do physical work in my job. But he bangs me and says: vote you stupid woman! Get yer hand up!

PAUL: I went past Clem Attlee House this morning.

DAVID: Oh yeah?

PAUL: [*to* ASIF] That's the Party headquarters. [*to* DAVID] There wasn't a pane of glass left in it. Is that to make the party more accessible?

STELLA: [*to* DAVID] How can you sit through those endless meetings with those mediocre bores going on?

DAVID: I've sometimes thought it my duty to see that things get done, in housing or education and so on. I thought big organisations could make small improvements in people's lives.

STELLA: [*to* AUDREY] He's disillusioned.

DAVID: I know now I should have started my own commune, my own school or—

AUDREY: I hate this rotten area now. It seems warm to me, waiting for trouble. All the different kinds of people they've got here, mixed up like bad ingredients. [*to* DAVID] You can feel it can't you? This'll be the year, you said. The summer.

DAVID: —or I should have set up a house for the homeless and distressed to run themselves. I lacked confidence, confidence.

AUDREY: [*to* ASIF] Did you see that sofa? Some beast left a sofa on the pavement outside the house. I can remember when the milkman had a horse. [*to* DAVID] Show Asif round the mansion.

DAVID: [*to* ASIF, *as they go*] A touch of damp sometimes collects at the top of the wall in your room. If it rains put your shoes under the bed.

[DAVID *and* ASIF *exit.*]

AUDREY: [*to* STELLA] I rang you and rang you.

STELLA: I stayed on in Paris.

AUDREY: Doing what, dear?

PAUL: Looking at galleries, reading, going to plays, strolling—

AUDREY: I'm leaving my job but I don't care, Stella.

PAUL: She does care. But you know what Dad said?

AUDREY: [*to* PAUL] Please turn on Asif's electric blanket.

PAUL: Dad said: You're just beginning. The elder Cato started to learn Greek at 80.

[EVA *comes in, bearing sandwiches.*]

EVA: Corned-beef's all right for Pakis, isn't it?

PAUL: [*leaving, to* STELLA] You kip in my bed. I'm taking the last train up London tonight. Louisa's Club has re-opened. I expect you went to the opening party. Asif did.

EVA: As long as Audrey gets her rent every week. To be honest I wouldn't be certain that...

STELLA: Eva you can tell, can't you? Asif smells... of money.

AUDREY: Oh yes.

EVA: I'd better cut the crusts off these, then.

PAUL: Don't tell Dad, but Asif's father used to make armaments. He's in ventilators now.

AUDREY: We're all right for the summer then.

PAUL: But he likes to turn the financial tap off and on, to keep ol' Asif gasping. I've known Asif so poor he had to borrow my shirt. A week later he'd fly to Venice still wearing it.

[*He goes.*]

AUDREY: [*to* STELLA] Stay a while, Stella.

STELLA: Till tomorrow, Mum.

EVA: Your father might be made redundant too.

AUDREY: We won't be able to keep up this house.

EVA: What d'you think of that?

STELLA: I haven't lived here for years.

EVA: When we were cleaning out your old room for Asif we found drugs on top of the curtain pelmet.

AUDREY: [*to* STELLA] You must have forgotten where you hid them.

EVA: She was never here, really. Out hitch-hiking.

AUDREY: You wanted new things, didn't you, love?

STELLA: I do now, all the time.

EVA: Most normal people don't run away from their mum and dad at 17.

STELLA: The end of the 60's, it was.

AUDREY: You went to Africa and India.

STELLA: And Russia. But none of it was to leave you. Neither of you should ever suggest it was, okay?

EVA: [*rising*] I've started something. Bye Aud.

AUDREY: Your friends from school still live in this road. Or they've bought houses in Dartford.

STELLA: I can't think of an explanation.

[ASIF, DAVID *and* PAUL *enter.*]

DAVID: [*to* ASIF] We'll make sure you're left in peace. We respect learning.

ASIF: [*to* AUDREY] There's two whole rooms full of books up there. [*to* DAVID] Have you read them all?

AUDREY: He used to be down here reading at five in the morning, before going to work, wearing gloves it was so cold. Now I don't let you start till six, do I?

ASIF: I bought my father a book once. It was in two volumes and it stayed on his desk for six months.

PAUL: [*to* DAVID] D'you think any of your learning's got you anywhere?

ASIF: Until one day Papa had a rage because my sister failed her law exam. He threw one volume at her and the other at a servant.

EVA: A servant?

ASIF: And Papa shouted, as the servant fled: let him see it! While I'm wearing out my eyes on books I'm losing money to keep this blasted rotten family going!

PAUL: [*to* DAVID] Unless they've stopped asking you to sweep up in that printer's you've given your life to.

AUDREY: He does the paper-work.

DAVID: Kafka wrote—

PAUL: [*to* AUDREY] I've seen him sweeping up.

DAVID: Kafka wrote: "A book must be an ice-axe to smash the sea frozen inside us."

EVA: Quiet a minute. I've got to go and I haven't heard what the servant said about the book. Asif.

ASIF: Illiterate. But with a bump now on his head. He was

my favourite servant. He brought me up. But if he
died they wouldn't tell me.

EVA: Why not? Why not?

DAVID: [*to* ASIF] You're a real student, at least.

AUDREY: You can't do wrong in his eyes. Our son's a bum,
you see.

DAVID: I didn't read anything until I was 28. I'd already
been working for thirteen years, thirteen years!

STELLA: What was it?

DAVID: The author had me in mind. "Midway this way of
life we're bound upon, I woke to find myself in a
dark wood, where the right road was wholly lost
and gone." I read it in the train between Sydenham
and London Bridge, the slowest journey in the
world. You have to stand for an hour in fetid air
with the point of an umbrella in your kidney.

EVA: You were a clerk in that tax office.

DAVID: "Where the right road was wholly lost—"

PAUL: Crap, in my opinion. South London's a zoo. Quotes
can't help you. Like everyone else round here now,
I live off my wits.

DAVID: But you live off mine, off mine.

PAUL: In so many ways armies have trampled over you
two. No one's going to make me redundant.

EVA: Difficult. Now go and lie down under my car.

STELLA: [*to* EVA] I thought Uncle Ted was going to buy you a
new Volvo?

EVA: He would. But I hardly use the car I've got, now
we've got the video. [*to* ASIF] You know, Ted my
husband says you won't find a better motor-
mechanic in Penge than this boy. He could have got
somewhere. [*to* AUDREY] Why ever did you let him
give it up? [*to* ASIF] Ted wasn't scared of starting
with nothing.

DAVID: Eva.

EVA: We own a central-heating firm now with eight
people under us.

DAVID: Isn't he laying four of them off?

AUDREY: Is he? Is he?
              [*Pause.*]
    EVA: [*to* ASIF] So if you want to see what England's really
              like, come out to Chislehurst sometime.
   ASIF: What is there?
  DAVID: Eva's rocks.
    EVA: Our big house. My lawn, my flowers, my trees. And
              my honeysuckle along the back wall.
  DAVID: Chislehurst, Kent. Where Marlowe wrote 'Hero
              and Leander'.
   ASIF: When was this?
  DAVID: May it was. 1593. 1593.
              [EVA *and* PAUL *go.*]
AUDREY: Eva. Eva. [*to* DAVID] It's not true that Ted's laying
              them off, is it?
  DAVID: Yes, it's true.
AUDREY: Don't tell me now. [*to* ASIF] Hot chocolate or some-
              thing else? Milk? [*to* DAVID] Wait a minute. I think
              I'd better know straight away.
  DAVID: [*to* AUDREY] I bumped into little Dennis who works
              for Ted.
 STELLA: [*to* ASIF] It's a miserable run-down area but I hope
              you get your work done. What are you studying?
   ASIF: I'd like you to come out with me tonight. [*Pause.*]
              All right, I'll persuade you later.
              [*He goes to his trunk.*]
AUDREY: David.
  DAVID: I bumped into Dennis. He's staying with the firm a
              bit longer. But Ted's practically bankrupt, practi-
              cally bankrupt.
AUDREY: You feel slightly they've been too proud with us,
              don't you? But we don't want them to suffer, do we?
  DAVID: They're on scuffed knees already.
AUDREY: Poor Eva. [*to* ASIF] I'll get your hot milk and bring it
              to you in bed.
   ASIF: Mrs Bareham. Tomorrow I must start to work.

AUDREY: Sorry, love?

ASIF: Tomorrow I may become a saint. But for tonight Paul's recommended a good club near here.

AUDREY: You're my new son, so you stay in. There's gangs that come down from the estate at night that wouldn't like you. I can't describe that estate to you.

STELLA: Isn't that because you haven't been there?

DAVID: She hasn't been to hell either.

[STELLA *kisses* AUDREY *and* DAVID *and they go.*]

STELLA: Walk up to Beckenham. There is a club. David Bowie used to take me there.

[*She laughs.*]

ASIF: Suppose I'm murdered on the way by frustrated working-class?

STELLA: Walk quickly.

ASIF: I think I'm going to like your family. I've been in England three years but I haven't got to know a real family yet. I intend to learn all about English life. Go right into it. And the summer's nearly here. I'll be able to study. I'll have no alternative here. Will I? I feel so happy in anticipation. I just want to laugh.

STELLA: Don't restrain yourself because of me, Asif.

ASIF: Not at anything specific. But only because I've wasted my life until now.

STELLA: Why have you encouraged Paul to waste his life?

ASIF: What?

SCENE TWO: A month later

The sound of a large motor-mower offstage. The French windows are open onto the garden. ASIF *comes in from the garden, wearing shorts and a bright shirt. He cuts a piece of cake and goes back into garden with it.* EVA *and* AUDREY *come in. They have been gardening.*

AUDREY: Dirt on you.
> [*She bangs the dirt off* EVA's *skirt.*]

EVA: What would you have done with that lawn if I hadn't brought that big mower up here?

AUDREY: I think I've got St. Vitus Dance.

EVA: Your David can't have pulled out a weed for years. Nor has Paul.

AUDREY: Where has he been the last three days?

EVA: I expect he's in trouble. Asif could have helped with the long grass instead of sitting in that deckchair.

AUDREY: I wouldn't ask him. David's got a name for him: Oblomov.
> [*Incomprehension from* EVA.]
>
> It's a dig.

EVA: He's only been here for a month.

AUDREY: Asif's idea of a working day is a lie-in, a walk, a lie down and an evening out before bed. In between — he eats. [*putting a chair out*] I've got to talk to you.

EVA: It's a sitting down subject? Oh dear. We've had a lovely day.

AUDREY: [*taking her hat off*] David says this hat is made of crushed canaries.

EVA: Ted bought it for me in Barcelona.

AUDREY: I only wear it for gardening. Now, you come here nearly every day now. Why? Why don't you say what's going on? Say what's gone wrong. Please.

EVA: We're nearly bankrupt. We're finished. Ted says—
> [ASIF *comes in from the garden. He goes to the far side of the room and sits.*]

AUDREY: How will we get that mower back to your car?

EVA: Leave it.

AUDREY: That monster.

EVA: Ted says he's going to sell my car. The recession's broken us in two. It's true. You could tell. Don't pretend.

AUDREY: Let's go into the kitchen.

EVA: He's stopped giving me money. To get me used to the situation. To help me appreciate the serious- ness of our decline. And I haven't got money of my own. How will I buy food to avoid starvation? I said to him.

AUDREY: Yes.

EVA: You lose a few pounds sterling and then a few pounds weight, he said, then I'll reconsider.

AUDREY: Bloody beast he is.

EVA: I sold the blender to the little woman who comes in to clean. Then I concentrated on his things. And some beautiful gifts people brought to our house when people came regular.

AUDREY: What's he say?

EVA: Of an evening he sits there with his accounts all over the mahogany table in the big lounge. If you tip-toe in and ask him anything he looks at you with a face like Christ with the nails going in.

AUDREY: You built that firm together. He's got no right.

EVA: The last five years I haven't been involved. It was successful once. It ran itself. I thought it would go on and on.

AUDREY: This morning I thought: now I'm unemployed I'll stay here in bed till David gets home. Our best days are gone.

EVA: Not mine.

AUDREY: What are you going to do? [*Pause.*] No, Eva. Not all that again.

EVA: Get the kettle on, love. [*She looks at* ASIF.] I'll have a think.

AUDREY: [*whispering*] And not with him. No Eva.

EVA: [*calling*] Asif!

AUDREY: No.

EVA: [*calling*] Would you like a drink?

[*Exit* AUDREY. EVA *goes to* ASIF.]

You're an engineer aren't you?

ASIF: Not at this rate.

EVA: I'm not lugging that lawn-mower home. You don't know anyone who'd buy it, do you?

ASIF: I know rich people in London with lawns, yes.

EVA: Don't do it as a favour.

ASIF: I told you, my father spoils me. But only in spurts. So I buy and sell and take a commission.

EVA: D'you like ponds? We must drive to Keston to see some.

ASIF: You've still got the car?

EVA: For now. You can drive it if you want.

ASIF: I wanted to say... I enjoyed our talk on Sunday.

EVA: Didn't I drink too much? You hardly said anything. I want to know your opinion.

ASIF: On what subject?

EVA: What else is there? Our country. Perhaps you don't want to embarrass me. D'you like England?

ASIF: Of course.

EVA: Be honest.

ASIF: I've lived elsewhere, you see. Karachi, Poona, Dubai — where the workers go off at six in cattle trucks and it's too hot to stand on the balcony. Places where nothing works; places where you go into prison and never come out if you don't bribe the right person. But I'm aware that Asian people are hounded and persecuted here.

EVA: Some.

ASIF: Your husband Ted turns off the TV when a black face appears.

EVA: Has Paul said that behind my back?

ASIF: Yes.

EVA: I'll sell the television. We used to know Jews. All sorts came to the house for dinner parties. Twenty people at a time. I'd wear dresses worth a hundred pounds.

ASIF: In Karachi, when my father's feeling hot-headed, he won't sit next to whites. Yet he was a pilot in the RAF. They gave him the MBE. You mustn't look for rationality.

EVA: So he's high-up?

ASIF: In Pakistan no one can touch him. The last time he came here someone spat on him. [*noticing her bracelet*] It's good I think.

> [EVA *takes her bracelet off.*]

EVA: Sell it. David gave it to me. I'm not old. I need money to enjoy myself.

> [ASIF *puts the bracelet in his pocket.*]

My sister's the only good person I know. She's given herself to her family. But she's never been happy.

> [EVA *picks up* ASIF's *text-book and opens it about a quarter of the way through.*]

What's the specific gravity of—?

> [ASIF *snatches the book and opens it.*]

There's half a bottle of brandy in my car. I'll tell Audrey we're going out so she doesn't cook.

ASIF: It's not a good idea to tell her.

EVA: She wouldn't be able to speak.

ASIF: She'd think we were kissing.

EVA: Join me in the car.

> [PAUL *enters.*]

EVA: Where've you been, naughty boy?

PAUL: You're not my mother.

EVA: At a party, I expect. Several parties. Over several days.

PAUL: [*to* ASIF] What a houseboat that randy Maria's got. I didn't realise. You've seen it haven't you?

EVA: What did you do on it?

PAUL: We swam on it. Danced on it. We did everything on it. In two days.

EVA: [*to* ASIF] Once this boy was like my son, when Aud was out at work.

PAUL: [*to* ASIF] The girls asked where you were.

EVA: Now he's gone hard.

PAUL: Have I?

EVA: And rough. You look like death warmed up with car-oil in your hair.

[PAUL *grabs* EVA's *hand and rubs it in her hair.*]

ASIF: Paul!

EVA: I'll get a bruise there.

[EVA *gets up to leave.*]

PAUL: [*yelling at her*] At least I don't collect horse-brasses!

[EVA *exits.*]

Stella says I'll have to leave this place.

ASIF: You've just got back.

PAUL: To fulfil my human potential, stupid.

ASIF: Is she doing that?

PAUL: She drove me round the East End in a borrowed silver Mercedes. Her place is chock-a-block with art objects. Round here they're fucking philistines. I'm skint, Asif. I want to get up London again.

ASIF: Whatever you do, you won't last long with that Chelsea crowd.

PAUL: I want Maria.

ASIF: You're a baby. She likes babies. For a week.

PAUL: Look at this.

[*He takes off his shirt. There are nasty marks on his back.*]

Those devil-fucking bitches whipped me. What's on the menu for tonight?

ASIF: I'm afraid I'm going out now.

PAUL: You're a poncy bastard.

ASIF: What?

PAUL: Well you are lately.

ASIF: I came here not to enjoy myself.

PAUL: I thought we'd have a time. You living out here with me.

ASIF: I'm past times.

[DAVID *enters, wearing his work suit.*]

PAUL: Sister Placidus.

[PAUL *goes and sits at the table.*]

DAVID: Oblomov. Are you going out?

ASIF: I'm not Russian.

DAVID: There's nowhere to go round here.

ASIF: But you're never cheerful when you get home from work.

DAVID: I used to hurl first editions at my wife. So things are improving.

ASIF: I think you're the gentlest person I've met. When I'm with you I realise I don't know anything.

[DAVID *nods at him.*]

What are you doing this evening?

DAVID: I'm reading a book about the earth's crust, the earth's crust. And there's a woman I visit. She has a little beard, like the younger Dostoevsky. Have you read Dostoevsky?

ASIF: No.

DAVID: What have you done? I said I'd wash her hair. She may show me her breasts again, as a late Christmas present. She's 51 and wants to die. She's entirely neglected; I love her and practise hypnotism on her. Where are you off to?

ASIF: Here and there.

DAVID: Eva will drive you here and there, will she? That's why she's outside.

ASIF: She's giving me a lift.

DAVID: What kind of lift? You'd better take care of her.

ASIF: What d'you mean?

DAVID: Of course you won't. Get lost.

[*Exit* ASIF.]

Your mother hates having a stranger in the house

now. Not that he's a bad boy. And we need the
money more than ever, after today.

PAUL: I want a beer.

DAVID: I've had the worst and best day of my life today and
your face is exhausting me. If you don't lie down I'll
have to.

PAUL: If I can't enjoy myself here I'll go back up London.

DAVID: You've become a commuter.

PAUL:: Say something serious to me for once.

DAVID: You've become a commuter.

PAUL: It's dirty and poor here. It's a leaving place.

DAVID: The city tires me and the country bores me. The
suburbs are ideal.

PAUL: For what?

DAVID: Catullus would have lived in the South London
suburbs. They're a genuine combination of middle-
class and working-class life. Bank-clerks, milkmen,
civil servants and labourers live side by side with
flourishing hedges between them. We have comfortable houses with gardens. We are neither
integrated nor alienated. Out here we live in peace,
indifferent to the rest of the world. We have no
sense of communal existence but we are tolerant,
not cruel. There's a kind of quiet gentle righteous-
ness about the suburbs that I like. And there's a
shallow cold smug decency about it which turns my
stomach, turns my stomach. But I think the
suburbs are a feature of English life that has
succeeded and deserves to endure for at least a
thousand years.

PAUL: Mum's scared to go out. There are gangs now.
Your party didn't make headway.

DAVID: And I've lost my job. Yes.

PAUL: Shall I put out the flags?

DAVID: Voluntary redundancy. It's ecstasy, almost ecstasy.

PAUL: Then celebrate for Christ's sake!

DAVID: I'll read for three hours before bed.

PAUL: How will you live?

DAVID: Without you. So cheaply.

PAUL: Yes. I want London. And a flat like Stella's.

[AUDREY *comes in.*]

DAVID: At 16 you were thrown out of school. Audrey, I've told him, and I want to tell you that today—

AUDREY: Did you see Asif and Eva go off together?

PAUL: I'm hungry.

DAVID: She's got the tea on.

AUDREY: You know that's where she is. With him.

DAVID: We've got no income now but everything will be all right! Good redundancy money, so I've finished—

AUDREY: Why does she get everything?

DAVID: —with insignificant toil.

AUDREY: Why does she? Why? And we lose our jobs.

DAVID: When Eva wants something she just takes it.

AUDREY: We've never done that.

DAVID: That's a virtue.

AUDREY: Don't talk about virtue. We've never taken! That's why we've never had anything. But to do that now, with him...

DAVID: Just when we thought everything was going wrong for her?

AUDREY: Don't make me say that.

DAVID: You envy her.

AUDREY: Yes. I envy her. I envy.

DAVID: You envy the wrong things.

AUDREY: Yes, yes, the wrong things. To you they're the wrong things: clothes, holidays, pictures on the wall. But to me they would have made all the difference. What's keeping us in South London now?

DAVID: Our love of the place.

AUDREY: Make up your mind David.

DAVID: About what?

AUDREY: About which place it is we're going to move to.

DAVID: All right.

AUDREY: Good.

SCENE THREE: A month later

AUDREY — *laying the table for a light meal: with various salads, cold meats, etc.* DAVID *is with her.*

DAVID: I think it's a good idea. A new life for us, in another place. A new house, in the countryside. On my redundancy money.
　　　　[*He starts to go.*]

AUDREY: David. You aren't knocking up or anything tonight, are you?

DAVID: I've done enough for the Labour Party. We'll see how they deal with the estate this summer.

AUDREY: There's disturbances up there. So stay in. Talk to me, fat-face.

DAVID: Let fat-face get up at five to read, and write his journal and commonplace book.

AUDREY: Five years ago you had a breakdown. Whatever it was. Rest, rest.

DAVID: I'd rather not be unconscious all my life.

AUDREY: You know what's happening here do you? Oblomov's gone out into the garden. And Eva's gone with him.

DAVID: I've got no time for all I want to think and study and do. How can they be in the garden? It's pouring with rain.

AUDREY: They've both got umbrellas. You're in charge. [*Pause.*] I'll be glad to move. Eva moved away from this area.

DAVID: To Chislehurst.

AUDREY: Up there it's another world. I need another world.

DAVID: True.

AUDREY: Don't I deserve another world?

DAVID: You've envied her too much.

AUDREY: With reason.

DAVID: No, no.

AUDREY: Her life has been a holiday. I've been a packer. We could have done better for ourselves.

DAVID: Put this house on the market.

AUDREY: You mean it?

DAVID: Let's get out.

AUDREY: Start getting those books in boxes.

[PAUL *and* STELLA *enter.*]

Stella.

DAVID: [*friendly*] What do you want, my love?

AUDREY: [*to* DAVID] Don't.

[*She kisses* STELLA.]

PAUL: I was out and about up London in the rain so I got her to drive me here.

AUDREY: We're just having our tea.

DAVID: Join us, join us.

AUDREY: Yes, I'll get more food out the fridge. Now, both of you, you mustn't mention anything to Eva.

PAUL: On what subject?

AUDREY: Any subject. Or I'll have your guts.

[AUDREY *exits.*]

DAVID: My, Stella, I thought you'd be teaching the language of Swift and Hazlitt to lupine German industrialists.

STELLA: Yes. I've been conjugating most of this week.

PAUL: It looked as if you'd been decorating.

DAVID: [*to* PAUL] Cut us some bread.

PAUL: [*indicating the bread*] Stel?

STELLA: Why can't we harass Auntie Eva?

DAVID: You should know their business has more or less gone down the toilet.

STELLA: Oh no.

PAUL: What's gone wrong?

[*They share the bread,* STELLA *and* DAVID, *taking a bite each.*]

DAVID: There was a time in England, the 60's, when everyone had to have a radiator in their front room and a brand new boiler in their open-plan kitchen. In short a central-heating epidemic hit the country. Ted and Eva couldn't have kids. But when did they have time to shag anyway? What with her up all hours doing the secretarial and Ted installing pipes? You'd see his van racing about the place. He'd wave but never had time to stop. People were giving him money. They bought modern cars and that mock house. 'Mango'.

PAUL: 'Limegrove'.

DAVID: Every time you visited, the walls were in a different place. Or they were extending the extension.

STELLA: And you pretended you couldn't find the toilet.

PAUL: Snob.

DAVID: Little prick, what do you know about how far they get above themselves, these people? And above you.

PAUL: They're our family.

DAVID: How they used to hurt your mother, waving that house in her face. She once begged Ted to take you on as an apprentice. He said: too lazy. They turn anti-union, these people; they talk about 'coloured' people. Finally they vote Tory, which is the worst thing, of course, the worst. And then they collapse like tents in the wind.

PAUL: They don't deserve it.

DAVID: It's happened. Because they made a mistake. They forgot that in England it's always them and us. Them and us. Nothing changes that. They tried to join them. And they've been destroyed. You can't cross that river. They're in Purgatory.

STELLA: Them and us.

PAUL: [*also imitating his father*] Purgatory.

STELLA: Those old words remind me of outside toilets. You still believe them?

DAVID: Not bitterly. But yes. I've lost interest in class. Astronomy is interesting.

STELLA: What am I?

DAVID: You?

STELLA: In this divided scheme?

PAUL: Tricky one, Dad.

STELLA: Them? Or us?

DAVID: Do you work?

STELLA: Occasionally.

DAVID: When you can't avoid it?

STELLA: Naturally.

DAVID: Doesn't that put you in a different position to ordinary people?

STELLA: In the same position, I would have thought.

DAVID: Ordinary people have to work. When they don't, they suffer. Because they take on obligations. I know you, Scorpion Stella. Feckless, independent, with contempt for ordinary people. Your smart London people don't understand the constraints of most people's lives. What they endure. So you're 'them' technically.

STELLA: Endurance. You just said endurance.

DAVID: Yes. And you will always take the easy way.

STELLA: Tell me. All the time you were reading Jack London upstairs or shouting in here about differentials with your square-shouldered Stalinist cronies, where was Mum?

DAVID: What?

STELLA: Where was she, geographically speaking?

PAUL: In the kitchen, I expect, geographically.

STELLA: Endurance.

DAVID: We love each other! We have a partnership. Why don't you bring a husband here, drifter? What do you know about profound sustained commitments to people, to people.

STELLA: What do you know about spin-dryers?

DAVID: We haven't got one.

PAUL: We have.

DAVID: Where is it?

PAUL: Mum knows.

STELLA: [*laughing*] Parity begins at home.

DAVID: Look at her. A conversational acupuncturist. No
        seriousness. For her, ideas are just fashions. She's
        made of neon.

STELLA: Why do I make you unhappy?

DAVID: Oh... [*to* PAUL] At 14 she reacted against my
        puritanism. [*to* STELLA] You were vigorous. You
        excited me. I took your education in hand. Sat with
        you every night at this table. Poured out my mind to
        you. And sent it out with you into the world.

STELLA: The day I left here, d'you remember, for college?

DAVID: Yes, yes.

STELLA: You gave me a book by William Morris. You wrote
        in it: Stella, your education is my only ambition and
        my only achievement.

DAVID: Ted took photographs. For an hour he respected
        me.

STELLA: So I went through it all. For you.

DAVID: But I wanted you to be a lecturer in a university. Or
        an M.P. Or a barrister. What's put you out to sea?

STELLA: Don't interfere with me.

DAVID: And do you think the tax-payer educated you just
        to enjoy films with sub-titles?

STELLA: Yes.

        [TED *appears at the other end of the room. He is
        wearing wet dirty overalls over his trousers and
        shirt.*]

TED: Just let me take off me trousers.

        [PAUL *goes to help him.*]

DAVID: [*to* STELLA] I miss these talks.

STELLA: Hallo, Uncle Ted.

DAVID: And you hardly come here now.

STELLA: Families — I hate you.

TED: Looking nice, Stella.

DAVID: Sit down, Ted. Your legs must be giving way with
        work.

TED: How do you know?

DAVID: They always are.

[AUDREY *comes in with food.*]

AUDREY: There you are, Ted. Get tucked in. Rest your legs.

STELLA: We were just talking about you, Uncle Ted.

TED: Saying what, my dear?

AUDREY: [*preparing him a plate of food*] That we haven't seen you for a long time. You've been so busy. You haven't had a minute.

TED: Eva's here every day, isn't she?

AUDREY: Oh yes, she comes over to us on the bus.

TED: I know how she gets here. [*indicating the food*] Lovely, Aud.

AUDREY: Want to wash your hands?

TED: [*picking up some cutlery*] I'll use these.

AUDREY: [*to the others, indicating the food*] Come on, what d'you want me to do, eat it for you and then burp as well?

TED: Where's this lodger I keep hearing about?

PAUL: I think he's in the garden.

AUDREY: We aren't certain.

TED: Pour me a drink, son. Got a job yet?

PAUL: Not yet, no.

TED: [*to* DAVID] Why don't you let me find Paul a job?

STELLA: I hear you're looking for bar-work yourself, Ted.

TED: I didn't say I'd offer this boy anything myself even if he had the last pair of arms in Orpington. But I know a desperate plumber out at Dartford who's after an apprentice.

PAUL: You work all the time.

TED: I sleep a five-hour night.

STELLA: Why, Uncle Ted?

TED: Stella, why don't you pass me a fat piece of cheese?

AUDREY: I'll do it.

TED: It's a good question. When me and Eva used to come back off our holidays I used to say there must be some way of stopping this endless working.

DAVID: It's easy. You just have to vote Tory. It isn't socialism that gave you blood-shot eyes.

AUDREY: He'll have indigestion in a minute, you big arse.

[EVA *and* ASIF *appear from the garden. Both are wet.*]

AUDREY: Oh God. Doesn't it ever stop coming down?

DAVID: Oblomov, meet Ted.

ASIF: Who?

EVA: Ted's my husband.

TED: [*to* ASIF] All right? [*to* DAVID] Oblomov's not a Paki name, is it?

ASIF: [*to* DAVID] I don't like it. Why the hell do you call me it?

DAVID: Didn't I leave the book on your bed?

ASIF: It's 485 pages long.

TED: [*to* PAUL] What are you going to do with yourself, son?

PAUL: I want to do something.

EVA: How's your girlfriend?

AUDREY: Maria. I haven't met her. No one has.

PAUL: No one will. I'm finished with those people.

ASIF: Why?

PAUL: We've got nothing in common.

[*He goes off.* AUDREY *follows him.*]

AUDREY: Paul — don't go up London again!

TED: He's a good boy.

DAVID: Asif — eat.

ASIF: Thanks. That's better.

TED: [*to* EVA] Shame you seem to have lost interest in our garden.

DAVID: Life treating you at all nicely, Ted?

TED: Tempted to ask something, David?

DAVID: I'll chew bread, chew bread.

TED: I want to tell someone something truthful. I feel as if I've been treading water for a year. Just to keep afloat. And all the time the tide's been taking me out to sea.

DAVID: I'm sorry.

TED: I'm beginning to feel the ol' water over my head. But I'm a bit of a fighter.

DAVID: Always.

TED: I won't let my business go. Because in the end I know this country won't let me down.

DAVID: You're sure of that?

TED: What a fool you are. If tough hard-working people like me can't survive, can't lift themselves up a little bit, who can? Soon there'll only be scum on the surface. Eva, pass the bread.

[DAVID *passes the bread to him.*]

ASIF: [*to* STELLA] We've got a friend in common. The bent lawyer, Saleem. He and I used to visit casinos together. Then he'd go off with girls.

[*As* ASIF *reaches for more food,* EVA *brushes his face lightly, not conspicuously.*]

EVA: An eyelash.

TED: [*to* ASIF] You're at one of our universities.

EVA: You know he is.

DAVID: [*to* TED] Have another bottle of brown. Do you have any idea what will happen to you?

[TED *uncaps the bottle and takes a long drink.*]

EVA: I'll be interested in hearing this.

ASIF: [*to* STELLA] I remember where I've seen you before. In the Horseshoe Casino in Knightsbridge. Saleem didn't introduce us but you were with him.

STELLA: It's possible.

TED: [*to* DAVID] You walked out through Kent lately?

DAVID: No. We must do it again.

TED: I've been on a job at Edenbridge. The fields and lanes at six in the morning. Paradise. You feel like stopping work, lying down in the grass and forgetting everything. I want to preserve it as it is forever. But sacrifices have to be made.

DAVID: Ah. Sacrifices.

TED: Sometimes you have to give things up in order to get other things, later on. I call it the two steps back and three forward theory, when you can't have what you can't afford. At the moment we're going back and everyone's panicking.

ASIF: [*to* STELLA] Who was this Oblomov, anyway?

EVA: Take me home, Ted.

TED: Am I ready to go?

          [EVA *begins to clear the plates.*]

          Eva may be suffering from exposure for all I know.
          But I've got a real problem. How to give four skilled
          men the sack. Old friends whose wives and kids I
          know. I believe in loyalty. I encourage it and they've
          never let me down, those men. Has anyone here
          had to sack someone?

DAVID: It's been done to me.

ASIF: [*to* STELLA] You don't see Saleem any more?

STELLA: What's the date of your exams?

TED: [*rising, indicating the bottle*] I expect you're hiding
          more of this in the kitchen. So there you are, com-
          pared with what I have to do, you're all laughing.

          [TED *goes out.* EVA *follows, with the plates.*]

STELLA: To answer your question. Oblomov's a landowner
          who won't get out of bed. A rich man destroyed by
          inertia. A fat vain lump of lard existing for nothing.
          [*to* DAVID] We are talking about the same book aren't
          we?

ASIF: That isn't what you think of me is it?

DAVID: I'm afraid my daughter has a sense of humour.

          [*Exit* DAVID.]

STELLA: [*preparing drinks*] I must go too.

ASIF: To work?

STELLA: Ted's always been an industrious turkey. It's Eva I
          pity. What could be worse than a woman in her
          situation?

ASIF: What about a woman in your situation?

STELLA: Why?

ASIF: First of all, I like you. I'm not against you. And my
          father has used prostitutes. I have. I don't see it
          morally. There's no point in Pakistanis looking at
          England morally — they would become insane.
          You have to make money, that's all. I know all those
          Chelsea people, the prostitutes and the gamblers.

Do you work much? The way of life, the clubs, the idiots, the drinking, that would bore you.

STELLA: That's why I make a living, not a fortune.

[EVA *comes in.*]

EVA: We're off now.

STELLA: All right Eva. Sorry.

[STELLA *leaves quickly.*]

EVA: What are you saying to her?

ASIF: Will I see you tomorrow?

EVA: Yes, yes.

ASIF: They don't mind you coming here every day?

EVA: It's all right, they think I'm having a breakdown. [*Pause.*] You've been like fresh air to me.

[TED *comes in.*]

TED: I'm out at Edenbridge again tomorrow. [*to* ASIF.] Eva makes delicious sandwiches. Rub my shoulder, love. She can do a massage too. What do you think of us all so far?

ASIF: I think there's plenty of opportunity for Asians in this country.

TED: That's true. Though I would put our people first.

ASIF: I hear you have a nice house.

TED: Yes. For some reason it's... no, it's everything to us.

EVA: [*to* ASIF] When we bought it, I remember thinking, standing in the garden: what good days we've got ahead of us. Didn't you Ted?

END OF ACT ONE

ACT TWO

SCENE ONE

ASIF *is sitting at his books. He is wearing a good suit.* EVA *comes in. She kisses him. He keeps working.*

EVA: Thank God you're here. Where've you been? Asif.

ASIF: You've got your black dress on.

EVA: Yes. The Mayor had it made for me. You like it?
 [ASIF *looks at the dress.*]

ASIF: Take it off.

EVA: This isn't America, Asif. We must have something to say first. [*Pause.*] You should tell me where you go. I can't keep ringing here. Has your father arrived in England?

ASIF: Last night I went to the casino in Knightsbridge. My friend Saleem lost fifteen hundred pounds, which he won back. I lost... five hundred.

EVA: Which is in their bank. You bloody fool. You could get a car for that.

ASIF: There'll be cars. All that. And I'll drive you where you want.

EVA: Why talk like this? What's happened?

ASIF: Kiss me.

EVA: Ted locked himself in the garden shed for the whole weekend. He spent two days down there. He wants peace of mind, poor man. I had to leave his food outside.

ASIF: I've got news too.

EVA: What am I going to do with him...?
 [ASIF *laughs.*]
 What news have you got, funny face?

ASIF: I've been with my father. He's lying in state at the Waldorf. And yesterday he changed everything. My suit and my whole life.

EVA: I guessed it. He's flown in from Pakistan to take you back to run the factory. Goodbye then.

[PAUL *enters.*]

PAUL: My dole cheque's come. Get the cards out, Asif.

EVA: In twenty-four hours Asif is going to take an exam.

PAUL: Let's get started, then.

ASIF: It's all right, Eva. I've decided that engineering doesn't excite me any more.

PAUL: What's exciting you now, Asif?

ASIF: Property.

PAUL: But you're not property are you, Auntie Eva? [*lying down*] I'm excited about sleep. Stroke me, Auntie Eva.

EVA: Baby. [*She strokes his hair.*] You're tired.

ASIF: Were you at the estate last night?

PAUL: Yes. Watching for fights.

ASIF: Anything?

PAUL: Plenty. It's hot and uneasy up there. People are just roaming about, waiting for it to start again. You Asians have got vigilante groups. The racists have got their units and the police appear to be away at the moment.

ASIF: Why 'you Asians'?

PAUL: It's good to see them organising and resisting. I thought you might feel cheered up.

ASIF: By shouting and stone throwing? Most English don't realise that the immigrants who came here are the scum of Pakistan: the sweepers, the peasants, the drivers. They've never seen toilets. They've given us all a bad reputation because they don't know how to behave. I couldn't talk to them there, except to give them orders. And I won't be solid with them here.

PAUL: Let's hope the English kick your proud brown arse right into the gutter, eh?

ASIF: There are other ways of achieving social peace. I've got some ideas. Prosperity is a great quietener, you know.

[PAUL *exits.*]

EVA: When are you going?

ASIF: I made it clear to Papa that his ventilators turn my stomach. It's a thirty mile drive to the factory on unmade roads. When he used to come home from work he'd collapse and say: I could hire out my stomach as a milkshake machine. All his life he's done the milkshake ride twice a day. He knows I hate the filth and noise of the factory. He's decided to invest here. In property. He's desperate to get his money out of that terrible country. The Russians are on the border and those religious fanatics want to advance the country into the eighth century. Papa's so suspicious of everyone else he's giving all the money to me. It's a matter of time before I'll be able to buy something. I'm staying, Eva.

EVA: I love looking at property.

ASIF: We're looking at property now.

EVA: What?

ASIF: They've talked about selling it. I'm going to make a good offer for this house. My father said: you want to buy a bijou place that wasn't built after the war. The English haven't done anything good since 1945.

EVA: Don't be daft.

ASIF: I want it.

EVA: I know what I'm saying. All my life I've looked at houses. Our parents used to take me and Aud to Chislehurst every Sunday as a treat. We'd walk backwards and forwards past the places. You'd see the backs of velvet chairs and people having breakfast by the window. We talked about it all the time, dreamt about it, but we never thought it was possible for people like us to live there.

ASIF: Is it possible, Eva?

EVA: I'll string myself up from the bannisters if we have to leave Chislehurst. Our mother worked in the

Post Office and we were brought up in a grubby place like this.

ASIF: These places are sturdy as tree trunks.

EVA: In my mother's old house they'd plastered a quarter of an inch of brown varnish on the doors. We'd splinter our nails on it. What would you know about miserable houses? You had your own tennis courts. And the servants were ball boys. I've seen enough old furniture to last me a lifetime.

ASIF: Where was this wretched house?

EVA: Up by the photocopied flats on the estate. You really want this place?

ASIF: Even more than I want you. [*Pause.*] With respect...

EVA: With respect what?

ASIF: I think you have a husband.
[*He gives her money.*]
You're like a shopgirl Eva. Get that hamster husband of yours out of his hutch at the end of the garden and screw money out of him.

EVA: You've got no understanding. Can't you see that things are coming back on us because Ted and me have had too much? It's all coming back on us!

ASIF: Don't be bloodless Eva. Get an evening job.
[*She attacks him and they fight.* PAUL *comes in and watches.*]

EVA: Where are you going?

ASIF: I have to stroke my father's cheque-writing hand.
[ASIF *exits.*]

EVA: Look at your hair, stupid.

PAUL: Why are you crying?

EVA: Why do you sleep in the day?

PAUL: Because I'm so active during the night-time.

EVA: Wiggling in clubs.

PAUL: No, no. Up the estate. The nights there seem to go on forever. We watch, we organise, and we beat the shit out of people.

EVA: Asif's got the right idea, the brown bastard. Respectability and effort. He's not worthless like you. You were always so quick, so bright...

PAUL: I know him. He uses women to invigorate himself. They're a challenge. Like wind-surfing.

[DAVID *enters.*]

EVA: Why does your dad look like he's just had all his teeth out?

PAUL: He's dieting.

DAVID: It's not a diet. It's a fast. So keep out of my way Eva. You're beginning to look like a fried steak.

EVA: I thought you'd gone vegetarian.

DAVID: It's not vanity. It's to induce extraordinary states of consciousness.

[AUDREY *enters, bringing tea and biscuits.*]

For example, in a vision I can see Mum carrying tea and biscuits.

AUDREY: Out of the way you big berk.

DAVID: Any break in the tranquil pattern, any breach of continuity, is an enlivening thing.

AUDREY: [*to* PAUL] You're here, are you?

DAVID: And from now on I want to think, not talk. Not talk.

AUDREY: [*to* PAUL] I've been hearing about the estate on the radio.

DAVID: Someone will get killed up there, won't they?

PAUL: Flats have been burnt out already.

EVA: With people in them?

PAUL: The people left quickly.

AUDREY: [*to* DAVID] Pour the tea before it gets hot.

DAVID: I've had a thought!

AUDREY: I want my lie down, so hurry up.

DAVID: Tea at this time of the afternoon. Anyone for a biscuit? What an extraordinary country this is! There can't be more than two or three people who actually have jobs now. And apart from Margaret Thatcher they all work for Ted. Why do we accept

it and drink tea? Look how placid and happy my
Audrey is, doing nothing.

EVA: What do you know, fat-arse?

DAVID: What do you say, Audrey?

AUDREY: I expect if I sit in this house any longer with nothing
to do but washing-up I'll deteriorate.

EVA: But you're going away. You talk about nothing else.

DAVID: At three in the morning she jumped out of bed and
started packing a box of old clothes.

AUDREY: Yes, we're having a party. I'm going to get merry
and then we're leaving London. Can't we burn
those books of yours 'stead of carrying them?

EVA: They've kept him quiet over the years. We should
have looked at them. We could have been cleverer,
Aud.

AUDREY: Us? We might as well not have gone to school. We
haven't done much with ourselves, have we?

EVA: I built up a business, didn't I?

AUDREY: So we must keep occupied now, doing whatever
small things there are to be done.

EVA: Why?

AUDREY: Otherwise we'll think about dying all the time. [*She
stares at* DAVID.] Looking at you now reminds me of it.

DAVID: You flatter me.

AUDREY: This fast. I'm getting a sandwich for you.

DAVID: No, no.

AUDREY: And I'm going to stuff it down your throat.

DAVID: Can't you let me live and let me be?

[AUDREY *goes out.*]

EVA: David. I want a word. [*to* PAUL] Go and look at my
car.

[PAUL *starts to leave, then stops.*]

PAUL: Ted sold your car, Eva.

DAVID: Go on.

[*Exit* PAUL.]

You don't have to touch me to talk.

EVA: Ted's being a bastard. He's starting to act oddly. David.

DAVID: I put fifty pounds in his hand to help start the business. July 1964 it was. For seventeen years he's flogged himself, providing employment and honest boilers. He's virtuous, virtuous in his own way. And now he's gone odd. I want to cry when I hear you say it.

[*He holds* EVA.]

I hear you've been selling off the rubbish you had in that house. Is there no furniture left, Eva?

EVA: There's a Persian rug I won't sell.

DAVID: It's on the wall. You'd better take a chair with you tonight.

EVA: Don't leave me, both of you.

DAVID: Got to.

EVA: No.

DAVID: Don't make a fuss.

EVA: I'm not. I'm telling you not to leave Sydenham. What will I do with myself? And him...

DAVID: I've no idea.

EVA: What have they got in Wales for Audrey? You can persuade her to stay. She'll soon forget the whole thing. I want you to do that. Otherwise I'll tell her about us.

DAVID: I'm too weak for this, for this.

EVA: What have I got to lose?

DAVID: It was over eight years ago.

EVA: I've excited you David.

DAVID: Terribly, terribly at times, my fault, stupid. Weakness, before I found myself.

EVA: David I'm warning you.

DAVID: Don't you love her?

EVA: That's why she can't go.

[AUDREY *comes in with a sandwich.*]

AUDREY: [*to* EVA] You'd better talk to that Asif tomorrow.

EVA: I can't face that journey home tonight.

AUDREY: I can't get on with Asif. I've never known a man to
          wear so much perfume.

EVA: People step all over your feet in those buses.

AUDREY: How d'you think I got to work all those years?

EVA: What?

AUDREY: Aeroplane? Will you tell Asif he's got to find some-
          where else to live?

> [EVA *goes to the door.* AUDREY *gives* DAVID *the
> sandwich.*]

          This will give you strength for the loft.

EVA: David.

DAVID: They're not my own radishes.

EVA: Don't forget what I said.

DAVID: I thought I didn't recognise them!

SCENE TWO

*Outside in the garden a party is in full swing. Sound of the
front door-bell ringing.* STELLA *comes in. The only light is
from the garden. She puts on a side-light. Most of the
furniture and books have been packed up. She picks up a
book.* PAUL *comes in with a bottle and is swigging from it.*

PAUL: You look good. [*Pause.*] Our last night in this house.
          You were eight when we came here.

STELLA: You won't remember the prefab we lived in before.

PAUL: Cardboard boxes on wheels.

STELLA: Dad kissed the floor when we got here. He got up
          and said 'mouldy'.

PAUL: I don't feel sad, Stella. I'm staying in South
          London.

STELLA: Do they know?

PAUL: They think I'm going to live in this house for a
          while. But I've got a permanent room in a place
          near Peckham.

STELLA: Live with me, until you find a better place in town.

PAUL: I'm not being romantic staying here. I just believe things can be bettered.

[AUDREY *comes in.*]

AUDREY: There's people at the door who think we're having a party.

PAUL: Aren't we?

AUDREY: Those roughs you know now.

PAUL: Good.

[*He goes to let them in.*]

AUDREY: Paul! No. My friends are here. The family. All the birds are in the nest.

PAUL: I'll give 'em the bum's rush then.

AUDREY: [*following him*] Yes, but nicely, Paul.

[PAUL *goes off, followed by* AUDREY. STELLA *remains with her book.* EVA *and* ASIF *come in.*]

EVA: I've always thought of my affairs as little holidays from the world.

ASIF: That's how I look at it.

[*They see* STELLA.]

ASIF: Eva's been telling me about her parties.

STELLA: Oh yes, strawberries and champagne.

EVA: Paul and his friend Dennis would put up lights and fix speakers in the garden.

STELLA: I never spoke. I danced alone for hours and hours.

EVA: [*to* ASIF] She wore long skirts made out of Aud's bed sheets and dyed green. By nine our drive was full of Rovers and Jags.

STELLA: And bank managers and local councillors. Tories.

EVA: All the crooks, bringing me gifts. We were spoilt.

STELLA: You two lovers wait here. I want to get you something.

[*She leaves quickly.*]

EVA: We've got honeysuckle all along the back wall in Chislehurst. It actually tastes of honey if you bite it in the right place. You have to know where that is.

You won't see it now. I'd have ended it myself. In time. I'd like a good cry, though.

ASIF: Please cry.

EVA: I wouldn't give you the pleasure. Here's a letter for you. Sorry, I picked it up and forgot about it.

ASIF: Exam results. You open it.

      [*She does so.*]

    Well?

EVA: Failed.

ASIF: Yes, but in which subjects?

EVA: In all subjects.

ASIF: Good. As expected. Don't tell anyone.

EVA: David'll want to know. Audrey says he's taken to you.

ASIF: They sneer at me, Stella and David.

EVA: From the first day David opened a book he used words to mock people who had more money than him. You're more sensible than him. And richer of course.

ASIF: But I don't have an intellectual background.

EVA: You have a white house on the beach with a squash court.

ASIF: But there, if you read a book by Bertrand Russell they think you're homosexual. One day my father was playing cards with his army friends. They snatched the book and passed it round, laughing. Then he aimed it at a lizard on the wall. I'll never go back there and be in their hands again.

EVA: Why should you? We'll give you the opportunity to do marvellous here.

      [STELLA *comes in with* PAUL. *She is opening a bottle of champagne.* PAUL *is carrying the glasses.*]

STELLA: Congratulations!

ASIF: [*screwing up the exam results*] I don't think I—

STELLA: You've bought our house.

ASIF: Yes, of course.

STELLA: Come on!

EVA: Drink to it!

ASIF: Yes, it's all mine. And I love it.

PAUL: Have you earned it?

EVA: It's his own initiative.

STELLA: [*patting his bum and holding it*] You look happy. What are you going to do now?

ASIF: I know you're not keen on Sydenham as a place, Stella. But I can't help having plans when I walk through this area. You could buy run-down houses, rip them out, refurbish them and install small businesses.

PAUL: The housing's falling down. And the people are run-down. Will you sell them? Or refurbish them first?

ASIF: I can help other Pakistanis get established here. This area's crying out for our business sense.

PAUL: This area's crying out.

EVA: [*noticing what* STELLA *is doing with* ASIF's *bum*] What you doing?

STELLA: I like a firm bum. But not one you'd be afraid to bite into. I'm speaking from experience.

EVA: [*to* ASIF] You're meant to be barbecueing.

ASIF: Oh yes.

[*Exit* ASIF.]

EVA: [*to* STELLA] Asif prays every day, you know.

PAUL: Bob and Maureen are here, Auntie. And Lesley. She's with that bloke whose teeth don't fit. And the central-heating superstar has arrived. In his Jesse James hat.

STELLA: Chislehurst's Mr Bovary.

PAUL: [*to* STELLA, *holding out his hand.*] Stel. You and me. Dance, eh?

[TED *comes in, in his hat.*]

TED: Which of you miseries is going to dance with me?

EVA: I should have sold that hat.

[TED *pulls* EVA *up.*]

TED: Let's get it over with. [*to* PAUL] I had a drink with

your old school mate Dennis this evening. He left the firm today. So I'm back doing the humping myself. But can I move? Smooth like a new wardrobe on castors.

> [*He sweeps* EVA *across the room and they waltz, closer to then further away from* PAUL *and* STELLA.]

PAUL: [*to* STELLA] I know where you get your money.

STELLA: What?

PAUL: [*to* TED] Go on, Uncle Ted!

> [TED *wiggles.*]

[*to* STELLA] Your living.

TED: [*shouting to* PAUL] Four years Dennis was with us. D'you remember you wanted his job!

PAUL: [*to* STELLA] I found out through those people I knew in London.

STELLA: You were shocked?

PAUL: It is shocking.

TED: [*to* PAUL] So Dennis has gone on the dole! At 23!

PAUL: [*to* STELLA] I bet prostitution's more insidious than you think. If you lead a worthless life you'll become worthless yourself.

STELLA: Prostitution's not meant to be a cause. Not meant to provide meaning in itself. It bought me time and intensity of experience. It paid for taxis and travel and meals. It has freed me from some tedious things. And now I'm going to New York.

PAUL: For good?

STELLA: To start a small distribution business. Books.

PAUL: Ted, you upset about Dennis?

> [TED *stops dancing.*]

TED: You think I'm not human? Your friend had a great future — once! But people have got to realise they can't have things unless they can afford them.

EVA: Ted.

TED: I'm exhausted.

EVA: I sold your cameras, the light meter, the projector, the screen, everything.

TED: It's my hobby!

EVA: We can't afford it.

TED: [*to* STELLA] She must be joking!

[DAVID *comes in, followed by* ASIF. DAVID *has a large, extraordinary piece of wood with him.*]

DAVID: Everyone's carousing in here. [*to* STELLA] He needs to cool down.

STELLA: Asif.

EVA: [*taking hold of him first*] Luckily Ted's put me in the mood for dancing.

PAUL: What's up?

ASIF: Two stupid women were talking about me. Janet and Maureen?

TED: They're the salt of Sydenham.

DAVID: It's no guarantee against idiocy.

PAUL: What happened?

DAVID: Ol' Oblomov was behind the tree cutting buns. Janet said: Asif's not bad looking. Maureen replies: no one that colour can be good looking, however good looking they are. Asif revealed himself and there were words.

TED: What kind of words?

DAVID: Sociological ones. Asif accused them of being working-class. Very funny, I thought.

EVA: [*to* ASIF] At parties you meet people you wouldn't normally trip over.

TED: There's all sorts of words I know.

EVA: 'Cept you'll save 'em.

TED: [*to* ASIF] You've got a cheeky mouth.

ASIF: [*to* PAUL] Shall I kick him out on his arse?

TED: Out where, old son?

ASIF: Out of my house.

TED: What house?

DAVID: I'm afraid you're treading on Asif's floorboards. [*to* EVA] Why the hell didn't you tell him, tell him?

TED: You bought this house with foreign money?

ASIF: Money's money.

TED: [*to* DAVID] And you just let him have it?

STELLA: [*to* ASIF] What will you do with it?

ASIF: It's perfect for conversion into two flats. That'll mean work and money. Because structurally the place will have to be altered. In the meantime I've got eight Indian students moving in.

EVA: Long as you keep up the garden.

ASIF: I'll turn the attic into another room, I think. And have a veranda built out there.

TED: [*to* DAVID] Where's your pride?

STELLA: Stay couth, Ted.

TED: Someone's got to say something. Our country's being nicked from us.

PAUL: By a businessman. What are you then, a ratcatcher?

TED: You're terrible, bloody cynical people. I can't believe it! You just don't care. You don't believe in yourselves. It's sickening.

ASIF: [*to* EVA] Do you want to cha-cha-cha?

TED: Don't touch him.

ASIF: What a silly man you are.

TED: No, I'm not a silly man. All my life I've given of my best. Others like me have. We don't want it taken away.

ASIF: What have you made of it? You know what the rich of Karachi say about you? I'll tell you. We say you are a Third World country. You know, under-developed. Your pound is worthless.

DAVID: Fuck the pound, we have the British Museum and the novel.

TED: He's pissing on us.

          [DAVID *smashes a glass on the table.*]

DAVID: If you fight any more I'll put this into the back of my hand.

TED: People don't want it to happen.

DAVID: Into the back of my hand.

          [TED *goes.*]

          What's wrong with being working-class? You're

working-class, Eva.

EVA: No, I'm not in any class now.

[ASIF *takes the piece of wood.*]

DAVID: Look at the grain of it. The shape. The colour.

ASIF: What do you think of academic achievement?

EVA: Asif.

DAVID: Not much now. Though my lack of it made me quarrelsome, resentful, perverse and obtuse for, oh about—

EVA: Twenty years at least.

ASIF: I failed my exams.

DAVID: [*touching the wood*] It's been worn smooth by the rain. Keep it.

ASIF: Where did you find it?

DAVID: It fell off the side of your new house. You see for us education was a lit-up gate to the future.

STELLA: [*to* ASIF] I'm sorry Ted insulted you.

ASIF: We know why the English say these things.

DAVID: Nothing stops my evening walk.

STELLA: [*to* DAVID] Take me with you.

DAVID: [*taking her arm*] Up to the Invisible Menders in the arcade.

PAUL: I'll take a picture of you two.

ASIF: I've bought a camera.

EVA: Fetch it. Paul, don't let Ted see it.

DAVID: Let's go, Stella, before your mother—

[AUDREY *comes in.*]

AUDREY: I'm having a party on me own out there, am I?

DAVID: No, Aud. Someone — go out!

AUDREY: You! Why is it always me who has to ask Lesley how the workmen left her loft?

EVA: [*to* PAUL] Go and ask Lesley how they left it. Then come and tell me.

AUDREY: [*to* PAUL *and* DAVID] Out!

[PAUL, DAVID *and* ASIF *go out to join the party.*]

I can sit down five minutes, can't I? Take off me shoes, Stel.

[STELLA *bends down and removes* AUDREY's *shoes.*]

EVA: While you're there, love.

[STELLA *removes* EVA's *shoes.*]

AUDREY: Let me put my feet into those.

[STELLA *puts* EVA's *shoes on* AUDREY's *feet.*]
What d'you think?

EVA: I'll say goodbye to them now, shall I?

AUDREY: [*to* STELLA] Kiss her for me, Stel. I can't reach.

EVA: We'll never come to this house again.

AUDREY: [*about* STELLA] She doesn't give a bum.

STELLA: That's right. Because I always imagined there could be some other way to live. Not shut in, in these families, in these endless streets where you hardly know anyone and you become afraid of everything. And you have a deadening job. And kids, as a matter of course. Goodbye to life. So I've managed to free myself from some of the things I was expected to do.

EVA: University.

AUDREY: She wore plimsolls and left before the end.

STELLA: I haven't found a new way of living, any successful way of living with other people. Or any belief, any strong interest beyond self-interest. I haven't found my place yet. But I will find direction, I will pick up the thread.

AUDREY: I feel so happy to be going to Wales.

EVA: You won't know anyone.

AUDREY: I don't want to know anyone. There was something you wanted to talk to me about.

EVA: I wanted you to have those shoes.

AUDREY: Right. Where's David...

[*She goes.*]

STELLA: Asif's full of energy now.

EVA: Yes, but it's over. Over now. And I'm glad. He should make the most of himself without anyone to worry about.

STELLA: Can't you try to be less generous towards men, Eva?
          [TED *appears behind them.*]

EVA: Asif's not lazy. Now he's bought the house he'll flourish and then—

STELLA: There's someone.

EVA: Asif.

TED: Edward John Spencer. [*He shows his crushed hat to* STELLA.] Guess which wog accidentally put their hoof into that?

STELLA: [*going*] Thank God your head wasn't in it.
          [*Exit* STELLA.]

TED: Home, eh?

EVA: I'm staying here tonight.

TED: We're coming back in the morning to help them anyway.

EVA: You'll be coming back, yes. I'll be waiting here for you. There's so much to do. Clothes to be packed up. They've left everything to the last minute.

TED: You don't like our home.

EVA: It's not that.

TED: You've let it go. There's dust on everything. The flower-beds are overgrown. The garage is full of old junk. You can't do anything heavy but you could—

EVA: Oh, can't you give me just one night to myself!
          [*Silence.*]

TED: When have I had a night to myself?

EVA: Not counting in the shed, you mean? So what if you haven't?

TED: Pardon?

EVA: There's no reason why we should both go down.

TED: All right.
          [*He goes out.* EVA *stands there. Music from the garden.*]

SCENE THREE

*The house has been stripped, though there might be some
items they've left behind for* ASIF. PAUL *and* STELLA *on
stage.* STELLA *is looking at a big map of Manhattan.* PAUL
*is sorting leaflets. There are some new, uncomfortable-
looking chairs, which* ASIF *has bought.*

PAUL: Have they located Dad?

STELLA: No.

PAUL: It's only when you participate in a place that you
feel you belong there.

STELLA: Why don't you collect your sayings for publication?
> [TED *comes in. He tries to lift a box. He is
> obviously in pain.*]

Ted.
> [*He stops, half bent over.* ASIF *comes in carrying a
> tape measure.* TED *glares at* ASIF *from his stooping
> position.*]

ASIF: I knew I'd forgotten something.
> [*Exit* ASIF. TED *straightens up.*]

TED: I won't be stopped by pain. Eva stayed here last
night.

STELLA: Yes.

TED: She didn't take anything to make her sleep, did
she?

PAUL: Oh no. She didn't sleep. We were all up.

TED: [*straining*] I'm happiest when I'm working.
> [*He goes out with the box.*]

PAUL: Sorry, I gotta do these, Stel. Essential information.
I'd want to see people got them, wouldn't I?

STELLA: [*giving him a tenner*] Will you have this?
> [PAUL *takes it and puts it away. He kisses her.*]

Have I got a line here, under this eye?

PAUL: [*tenderly*] A trench, Stella, under that one. What
does it matter, soon you'll be in New York.
> [ASIF *comes in with his notebook and tape
> measure.*]

STELLA: I'll be staying right there for a few weeks. [*She points to the map.*] The Chelsea Hotel.

ASIF: Can you have more than one hangover at a time?

STELLA: Then I'll move into an apartment on the Upper East Side. It's got three big rooms. Friends found it for me. There it is. By the Whitney. That's Central Park.

ASIF: Can you have three hangovers?

PAUL: Stella will know.

ASIF: Despite dizziness, this house is the beginning of my empire. Hold this, someone. I think I'm going to be an expansionist.

> [*And he whips the tape out of its drum.* PAUL *ignores* ASIF's *offered end of the tape measure.* STELLA *takes it and helps him to measure the floor.*]

PAUL: [*holding a leaflet in front of* STELLA] There's a public meeting tonight, about the estate. The police are going to meet the tenants. All summer it's been blood and glass and now those lumpen racists are holding weekly rallies in the middle of the estate. It'll be an energetic meeting. Most of us are only going in order to walk out.

STELLA: Will you be walking out, Asif?

ASIF: All the time they're exercising I'll be building.

STELLA: You're going into construction?

ASIF: This floor could be sanded and polished, couldn't it?

PAUL: Do your student tenants know you're bringing them to live in the middle of a racial whirlpool?

ASIF: The whirlpool is between your ears. And we don't need your help. We'll protect ourselves against boots with our brains. We won't be on the street because we'll be in cars. We won't be throwing bricks because we'll be building houses with them. They won't abuse us in factories because we'll own the factories and we'll sack people.

PAUL: Will everyone own factories or only those of you with wealthy fathers in Western-supported fascist countries?

[TED *comes back in.*]

TED: [*to* PAUL] It's nearly all in.

ASIF: [*to* PAUL] You're negative. And you've got no power. You don't count.

TED: Get hold of the other end of this, son.

ASIF: This house lacks a garage.

TED: [*to* PAUL] Come on.

STELLA: There's no room for a garage.

ASIF: I've just measured it. You could lay a path at the side of the house and build a garage round the back.

PAUL: Where the lawn is now?

TED: I stuck those rose bushes in that earth years ago. You helped me Stel, wearing yellow Wellington boots.

STELLA: It would raise the value of the place.

[PAUL *and* TED *go off with a box,* PAUL *pushing* TED.]

ASIF: Aren't you having dinner with me tonight?

STELLA: You'll be building the future, surely?

ASIF: Not all evening. I've rented a flat near you, where I'll be living. My London friends are only interested in sex and money. I want to go to galleries and concerts. You can tell me what to read. What do you think of Chekhov?

[AUDREY *and* EVA *come in.*]

EVA: If your ankles are swollen sit down.

AUDREY: Where?

[*She sits in one of the new chairs.*]

EVA: Leave some of that old furniture here and in a few months Asif'll throw it on the fire.

AUDREY: On the fire?

ASIF: But I'll have central-heating.

[TED *comes back in.*]

AUDREY: Where's David?

TED: On licensed premises.

ASIF: Are you busy at the moment, Ted?

TED: I'm always busy. You always busy? I don't rely on moving furniture for a living.

STELLA: Not yet, Uncle Ted.

TED: If it came to it I'd move furniture with a will. I'd soon have a fleet of vans roaring across England. Ted's Transport. Unlike you, I can't appreciate sculpture. But I can build a cupboard in a week-end take out your fireplace and have the strength left over to install a radiator.

ASIF: I thought I'd have central-heating installed here.

TED: It's a thought and a half.

ASIF: Interested?

TED: One more box.

[TED *goes off with a box.* DAVID *comes in. He is drunk.*]

DAVID: [*to* STELLA] I've sinned.

[STELLA *hugs him.*]

I've eaten meat, taken alcohol and used hypnotism on a political opponent.

STELLA: Why Dad?

DAVID: Not being limited by rigid principles, you see. And I've been round giving the farewell finger to my comrades and enemies in the Labour Party. They don't like my son. Apparently our Paul doesn't embody the decent urges of ordinary people. True. People like him may turn out to be dangerous changers of things. But political and moral radicalism is a dead duck at the polls because the electors are vegetarian. [*He looks round.*] Everything's gone.

AUDREY: How d'you get out of these chairs?

EVA: Asif knows.

[ASIF *helps her.*]

DAVID: [*to* AUDREY] In the van, love.

[PAUL *comes in, carrying his few possessions, and the leaflets.*]

PAUL: I'm going to say goodbye and then I'm going to turn round and walk out quickly. Goodbye.

[*He starts to walk out. Someone grabs him.*]

It's all right, I've got a room, I can dress myself and everything.

AUDREY: You can't! Stella, take him up London with you! Please, Stel.

STELLA: Put your one shirt in my car and get in, Paul.

AUDREY: Yes, Paul.

EVA: Go with her!

STELLA: We'll have time to talk about your future. I'd love you to be with me.

AUDREY: There's nothing here! What a place it's become — violent, dirty! The people are filthy dirt!

PAUL: They're not, not particularly.

AUDREY: Stop him, someone.

ASIF: He's caught an infantile disease.

PAUL: Families are divisive anyway. Why care for someone more because they came out of the same hole as you?

[*He goes.*]

DAVID: [*to* ASIF] There's a danger the water-tank will burst.

ASIF: Is it old?

DAVID: It's like rice-paper. Have a look at it.

ASIF: When?

DAVID: Right away if I were you. Right away.

[ASIF *goes.*]

EVA: [*to* AUDREY] Come on. [*to* TED] Ted.

TED: Give us that arm.

AUDREY: I've lived here all my life.

[TED, AUDREY *and* EVA *go off.*]

DAVID: Stella.

STELLA: You look as if you're about to give advice. Try not to.

DAVID: Tell me what you're going to do with yourself. What have I made of you?

STELLA: I'm a swimmer, reader and occasional big eater.

DAVID: That's how I was.

STELLA: Will you miss Eva?

DAVID: Should I?

STELLA: I wondered.

DAVID: No, I won't.

STELLA: You haven't always been a holy man.

DAVID: By the way, what's your age?

STELLA: Twenty-eight.

DAVID: Twenty-eight. It's a superb number. The completion of a lunar rhythm you know, a lunar rhythm.

STELLA: That's advice, not science.

DAVID: Oh yes, yes.

EVA: [*off*] They're going!

STELLA: Talk to Mum in Wales.

EVA: [*off*] David!

DAVID: There'll be no one else, will there?
[*He goes.*]

DAVID: [*off, shouting to* STELLA] Some things have more value than other things!
[EVA *comes in.*]

EVA: Go and wave! Quickly! I feel too faint. Quickly!
[STELLA *runs off. Pause.* ASIF *comes in, filthy and with cobwebs on him from the attic.*]

ASIF: They've gone?
[EVA *nods.*]
Let me say goodbye!
[*But* EVA *takes his hand and holds him.*]
Eva! There's nothing wrong with the tank.

EVA: 'Course not.

ASIF: You know, the rooms are echoing. When you walk round upstairs you hear nothing but yourself.
[ASIF *frees himself from her.* TED *comes in.*]

TED: They're away. David's driving. [*Silence.*] About this heating. When d'you want to discuss it?

ASIF: Next week.

TED: Right. [*to* EVA] Let's leave him to his palace.

EVA: Yes. Goodbye Asif.

TED: [*to* ASIF] I'll be in touch. Come over and have a drink.

ASIF: Okay.

TED: And a bite to eat. You can see the garden and Eva can do you an Indian.

ASIF: What?

TED: Whenever she makes something spicy she says she's doing an Indian.

EVA: [*to* TED] What's made you nice? What's made you so nice all of a sudden?

ASIF: Business.

TED: [*laughing*] It's not the biggest job I've had. I expect you've got mates with property, though.

ASIF: Oh yes.

TED: [*to* EVA] There you are. That's pleased me, love. What's the matter?

EVA: Nothing. Nothing's the matter.

THE END